MW00917961

The Safe House

The Internet Password Organizer Disguised as a Novel

Hidden in Plain Sight Volume 2

End lost password frustrations with this simple (but extremely useful) pocket-sized password organizer.

FastForwardPublishing.com

ISBN 10: 150553559X
ISBN 13: 9781505535594

TABLE OF CONTENTS

Tips for Using this Book

Enter your account and password information in the spaces provided (organized in alphabetical order for easy retrieval):

Title: TWITTER	Password Change	Date
URL: Twitter.com		
Log in: @scottfroth		
Password/Pin: %Mbf12003w5!		
Notes/Hints/Security Question		
Who was my best friend in 2003?		

Store the log in a location that is easy for you to access for

1. Looking up a forgotten password
2. Adding in a new account/password
3. Changing/updating a password

Make sure that the easy access to you is not easy access or intuitive to anybody else. For example file it under "S" for "security" or "F" for "find it" as opposed to "P" for password. Or put it in between some other books on a shelf. Even though this book is cleverly disguised, avoid keeping it in sight on your desk or in your laptop bag.

Tips for a Strong & Effective Password

A good password is an important first step to defending against intruders and imposters. Here are some tips to make sure your password does the best possible job.

1. Make your password hard to guess/hack, but easy to remember (see tip 7).

2. Make your passwords as long as possible (minimum 8 characters).

3. Use numbers, a combination of upper and lower case letters, and symbols (e.g., #, ^, &, etc.).

4. Avoid "dictionary" words. If a word is in the dictionary, it is easier to identify by hackers.

5. Don't use a password that includes your name or company name.

6. Use a randomized series of characters that include a mix of letters, numbers and symbols.

7. Consider using the "Sentence Tactic" for developing a strong password:

   a) Pick a sentence that you can easily remember; for example: My best friend in 2003 was Shawn

   b) Take the first letter of each word in the sentence: Mbfi2003wS

c) Replace some of those letters with numbers: Mbf12003w5 ("i" becomes "1" and "S" becomes "5")

d) Add in some punctuation (or a symbol or two): %Mbf12003w5!

e) You have a strong password that is relatively easy to remember

Here are a few other tips to help you protect your passwords

1. Use multiple passwords.

2. Don't post a password in plain sight (e.g., sticky note on your monitor). Use this book and keep it in a non-obvious place (even though it is cleverly camouflaged).

3. Make sure that your operating system is up-to-date and that you're using up-to-date anti-malware software.

4. Don't give your password to anybody.

A

Title:	Password Change	Date
URL:		
Log in:		
Password/Pin:		
Notes/Hints/Security Question		

Title:	Password Change	Date
URL:		
Log in:		
Password/Pin:		
Notes/Hints/Security Question		

Title:	Password Change	Date
URL:		
Log in:		
Password/Pin:		
Notes/Hints/Security Question		

Title:	Password Change	Date
URL:		
Log in:		
Password/Pin:		
Notes/Hints/Security Question		

Title:	Password Change	Date
URL:		
Log in:		
Password/Pin:		
Notes/Hints/Security Question		

Title:	Password Change	Date
URL:		
Log in:		
Password/Pin:		
Notes/Hints/Security Question		

B

Title:	Password Change	Date
URL:		
Log in:		
Password/Pin:		
Notes/Hints/Security Question		

Title:	Password Change	Date
URL:		
Log in:		
Password/Pin:		
Notes/Hints/Security Question		

Title:	Password Change	Date
URL:		
Log in:		
Password/Pin:		
Notes/Hints/Security Question		

Title:	Password Change	Date
URL:		
Log in:		
Password/Pin:		
Notes/Hints/Security Question		

Title:	Password Change	Date
URL:		
Log in:		
Password/Pin:		
Notes/Hints/Security Question		

Title:	Password Change	Date
URL:		
Log in:		
Password/Pin:		
Notes/Hints/Security Question		

C

Title:	Password Change	Date
URL:		
Log in:		
Password/Pin:		
Notes/Hints/Security Question		

Title:	Password Change	Date
URL:		
Log in:		
Password/Pin:		
Notes/Hints/Security Question		

Title:	Password Change	Date
URL:		
Log in:		
Password/Pin:		
Notes/Hints/Security Question		

Title:	Password Change	Date
URL:		
Log in:		
Password/Pin:		
Notes/Hints/Security Question		

Title:	Password Change	Date
URL:		
Log in:		
Password/Pin:		
Notes/Hints/Security Question		

Title:	Password Change	Date
URL:		
Log in:		
Password/Pin:		
Notes/Hints/Security Question		

D

Title:	Password Change	Date
URL:		
Log in:		
Password/Pin:		
Notes/Hints/Security Question		

Title:	Password Change	Date
URL:		
Log in:		
Password/Pin:		
Notes/Hints/Security Question		

Title:	Password Change	Date
URL:		
Log in:		
Password/Pin:		
Notes/Hints/Security Question		

Title:	Password Change	Date
URL:		
Log in:		
Password/Pin:		
Notes/Hints/Security Question		

Title:	Password Change	Date
URL:		
Log in:		
Password/Pin:		
Notes/Hints/Security Question		

Title:	Password Change	Date
URL:		
Log in:		
Password/Pin:		
Notes/Hints/Security Question		

E

Title:	Password Change	Date
URL:		
Log in:		
Password/Pin:		
Notes/Hints/Security Question		

Title:	Password Change	Date
URL:		
Log in:		
Password/Pin:		
Notes/Hints/Security Question		

Title:	Password Change	Date
URL:		
Log in:		
Password/Pin:		
Notes/Hints/Security Question		

Title:	Password Change	Date
URL:		
Log in:		
Password/Pin:		
Notes/Hints/Security Question		

Title:	Password Change	Date
URL:		
Log in:		
Password/Pin:		
Notes/Hints/Security Question		

Title:	Password Change	Date
URL:		
Log in:		
Password/Pin:		
Notes/Hints/Security Question		

F

Title:	Password Change	Date
URL:		
Log in:		
Password/Pin:		
Notes/Hints/Security Question		

Title:	Password Change	Date
URL:		
Log in:		
Password/Pin:		
Notes/Hints/Security Question		

Title:	Password Change	Date
URL:		
Log in:		
Password/Pin:		
Notes/Hints/Security Question		

Title:	Password Change	Date
URL:		
Log in:		
Password/Pin:		
Notes/Hints/Security Question		

Title:	Password Change	Date
URL:		
Log in:		
Password/Pin:		
Notes/Hints/Security Question		

Title:	Password Change	Date
URL:		
Log in:		
Password/Pin:		
Notes/Hints/Security Question		

G

Title:	Password Change	Date
URL:		
Log in:		
Password/Pin:		
Notes/Hints/Security Question		

Title:	Password Change	Date
URL:		
Log in:		
Password/Pin:		
Notes/Hints/Security Question		

Title:	Password Change	Date
URL:		
Log in:		
Password/Pin:		
Notes/Hints/Security Question		

Title:	Password Change	Date
URL:		
Log in:		
Password/Pin:		
Notes/Hints/Security Question		

Title:	Password Change	Date
URL:		
Log in:		
Password/Pin:		
Notes/Hints/Security Question		

Title:	Password Change	Date
URL:		
Log in:		
Password/Pin:		
Notes/Hints/Security Question		

H

Title:	Password Change	Date
URL:		
Log in:		
Password/Pin:		
Notes/Hints/Security Question		

Title:	Password Change	Date
URL:		
Log in:		
Password/Pin:		
Notes/Hints/Security Question		

Title:	Password Change	Date
URL:		
Log in:		
Password/Pin:		
Notes/Hints/Security Question		

Title:	Password Change	Date
URL:		
Log in:		
Password/Pin:		
Notes/Hints/Security Question		

Title:	Password Change	Date
URL:		
Log in:		
Password/Pin:		
Notes/Hints/Security Question		

Title:	Password Change	Date
URL:		
Log in:		
Password/Pin:		
Notes/Hints/Security Question		

Title:		Password Change	Date
URL:			
Log in:			
Password/Pin:			
Notes/Hints/Security Question			

Title:		Password Change	Date
URL:			
Log in:			
Password/Pin:			
Notes/Hints/Security Question			

Title:	Password Change	Date
URL:		
Log in:		
Password/Pin:		
Notes/Hints/Security Question		

Title:	Password Change	Date
URL:		
Log in:		
Password/Pin:		
Notes/Hints/Security Question		

Title:	Password Change	Date
URL:		
Log in:		
Password/Pin:		
Notes/Hints/Security Question		

Title:	Password Change	Date
URL:		
Log in:		
Password/Pin:		
Notes/Hints/Security Question		

J

Title:	Password Change	Date
URL:		
Log in:		
Password/Pin:		
Notes/Hints/Security Question		

Title:	Password Change	Date
URL:		
Log in:		
Password/Pin:		
Notes/Hints/Security Question		

Title:	Password Change	Date
URL:		
Log in:		
Password/Pin:		
Notes/Hints/Security Question		

Title:	Password Change	Date
URL:		
Log in:		
Password/Pin:		
Notes/Hints/Security Question		

Title:	Password Change	Date
URL:		
Log in:		
Password/Pin:		
Notes/Hints/Security Question		

Title:	Password Change	Date
URL:		
Log in:		
Password/Pin:		
Notes/Hints/Security Question		

K

Title:	Password Change	Date
URL:		
Log in:		
Password/Pin:		
Notes/Hints/Security Question		

Title:	Password Change	Date
URL:		
Log in:		
Password/Pin:		
Notes/Hints/Security Question		

Title:	Password Change	Date
URL:		
Log in:		
Password/Pin:		
Notes/Hints/Security Question		

Title:	Password Change	Date
URL:		
Log in:		
Password/Pin:		
Notes/Hints/Security Question		

Title:	Password Change	Date
URL:		
Log in:		
Password/Pin:		
Notes/Hints/Security Question		

Title:	Password Change	Date
URL:		
Log in:		
Password/Pin:		
Notes/Hints/Security Question		

L

Title:	Password Change	Date
URL:		
Log in:		
Password/Pin:		
Notes/Hints/Security Question		

Title:	Password Change	Date
URL:		
Log in:		
Password/Pin:		
Notes/Hints/Security Question		

Title:	Password Change	Date
URL:		
Log in:		
Password/Pin:		
Notes/Hints/Security Question		

Title:	Password Change	Date
URL:		
Log in:		
Password/Pin:		
Notes/Hints/Security Question		

Title:	Password Change	Date
URL:		
Log in:		
Password/Pin:		
Notes/Hints/Security Question		

Title:	Password Change	Date
URL:		
Log in:		
Password/Pin:		
Notes/Hints/Security Question		

M

Title:	Password Change	Date
URL:		
Log in:		
Password/Pin:		
Notes/Hints/Security Question		

Title:	Password Change	Date
URL:		
Log in:		
Password/Pin:		
Notes/Hints/Security Question		

Title:	Password Change	Date
URL:		
Log in:		
Password/Pin:		
Notes/Hints/Security Question		

Title:	Password Change	Date
URL:		
Log in:		
Password/Pin:		
Notes/Hints/Security Question		

Title:	Password Change	Date
URL:		
Log in:		
Password/Pin:		
Notes/Hints/Security Question		

Title:	Password Change	Date
URL:		
Log in:		
Password/Pin:		
Notes/Hints/Security Question		

N

Title:	Password Change	Date
URL:		
Log in:		
Password/Pin:		
Notes/Hints/Security Question		

Title:	Password Change	Date
URL:		
Log in:		
Password/Pin:		
Notes/Hints/Security Question		

Title:		Password Change	Date
URL:			
Log in:			
Password/Pin:			
Notes/Hints/Security Question			

Title:		Password Change	Date
URL:			
Log in:			
Password/Pin:			
Notes/Hints/Security Question			

Title:	Password Change	Date
URL:		
Log in:		
Password/Pin:		
Notes/Hints/Security Question		

Title:	Password Change	Date
URL:		
Log in:		
Password/Pin:		
Notes/Hints/Security Question		

O

Title:	Password Change	Date
URL:		
Log in:		
Password/Pin:		
Notes/Hints/Security Question		

Title:	Password Change	Date
URL:		
Log in:		
Password/Pin:		
Notes/Hints/Security Question		

Title:	Password Change	Date
URL:		
Log in:		
Password/Pin:		
Notes/Hints/Security Question		

Title:	Password Change	Date
URL:		
Log in:		
Password/Pin:		
Notes/Hints/Security Question		

Title:	Password Change	Date
URL:		
Log in:		
Password/Pin:		
Notes/Hints/Security Question		

Title:	Password Change	Date
URL:		
Log in:		
Password/Pin:		
Notes/Hints/Security Question		

P

Title:	Password Change	Date
URL:		
Log in:		
Password/Pin:		
Notes/Hints/Security Question		

Title:	Password Change	Date
URL:		
Log in:		
Password/Pin:		
Notes/Hints/Security Question		

Title:		Password Change	Date
URL:			
Log in:			
Password/Pin:			
Notes/Hints/Security Question			

Title:		Password Change	Date
URL:			
Log in:			
Password/Pin:			
Notes/Hints/Security Question			

Title:	Password Change	Date
URL:		
Log in:		
Password/Pin:		
Notes/Hints/Security Question		

Title:	Password Change	Date
URL:		
Log in:		
Password/Pin:		
Notes/Hints/Security Question		

Q

Title:	Password Change	Date
URL:		
Log in:		
Password/Pin:		
Notes/Hints/Security Question		

Title:	Password Change	Date
URL:		
Log in:		
Password/Pin:		
Notes/Hints/Security Question		

Title:	Password Change	Date
URL:		
Log in:		
Password/Pin:		
Notes/Hints/Security Question		

Title:	Password Change	Date
URL:		
Log in:		
Password/Pin:		
Notes/Hints/Security Question		

Title:	Password Change	Date
URL:		
Log in:		
Password/Pin:		
Notes/Hints/Security Question		

Title:	Password Change	Date
URL:		
Log in:		
Password/Pin:		
Notes/Hints/Security Question		

R

Title:	Password Change	Date
URL:		
Log in:		
Password/Pin:		
Notes/Hints/Security Question		

Title:	Password Change	Date
URL:		
Log in:		
Password/Pin:		
Notes/Hints/Security Question		

Title:	Password Change	Date
URL:		
Log in:		
Password/Pin:		
Notes/Hints/Security Question		

Title:	Password Change	Date
URL:		
Log in:		
Password/Pin:		
Notes/Hints/Security Question		

Title:	Password Change	Date
URL:		
Log in:		
Password/Pin:		
Notes/Hints/Security Question		

Title:	Password Change	Date
URL:		
Log in:		
Password/Pin:		
Notes/Hints/Security Question		

S

Title:	Password Change	Date
URL:		
Log in:		
Password/Pin:		
Notes/Hints/Security Question		

Title:	Password Change	Date
URL:		
Log in:		
Password/Pin:		
Notes/Hints/Security Question		

Title:	Password Change	Date
URL:		
Log in:		
Password/Pin:		
Notes/Hints/Security Question		

Title:	Password Change	Date
URL:		
Log in:		
Password/Pin:		
Notes/Hints/Security Question		

Title:	Password Change	Date
URL:		
Log in:		
Password/Pin:		
Notes/Hints/Security Question		

Title:	Password Change	Date
URL:		
Log in:		
Password/Pin:		
Notes/Hints/Security Question		

T

Title:	Password Change	Date
URL:		
Log in:		
Password/Pin:		
Notes/Hints/Security Question		

Title:	Password Change	Date
URL:		
Log in:		
Password/Pin:		
Notes/Hints/Security Question		

Title:	Password Change	Date
URL:		
Log in:		
Password/Pin:		
Notes/Hints/Security Question		

Title:	Password Change	Date
URL:		
Log in:		
Password/Pin:		
Notes/Hints/Security Question		

Title:	Password Change	Date
URL:		
Log in:		
Password/Pin:		
Notes/Hints/Security Question		

Title:	Password Change	Date
URL:		
Log in:		
Password/Pin:		
Notes/Hints/Security Question		

U

Title:	Password Change	Date
URL:		
Log in:		
Password/Pin:		
Notes/Hints/Security Question		

Title:	Password Change	Date
URL:		
Log in:		
Password/Pin:		
Notes/Hints/Security Question		

Title:	Password Change	Date
URL:		
Log in:		
Password/Pin:		
Notes/Hints/Security Question		

Title:	Password Change	Date
URL:		
Log in:		
Password/Pin:		
Notes/Hints/Security Question		

Title:	Password Change	Date
URL:		
Log in:		
Password/Pin:		
Notes/Hints/Security Question		

Title:	Password Change	Date
URL:		
Log in:		
Password/Pin:		
Notes/Hints/Security Question		

V

Title:	Password Change	Date
URL:		
Log in:		
Password/Pin:		
Notes/Hints/Security Question		

Title:	Password Change	Date
URL:		
Log in:		
Password/Pin:		
Notes/Hints/Security Question		

Title:	Password Change	Date
URL:		
Log in:		
Password/Pin:		
Notes/Hints/Security Question		

Title:	Password Change	Date
URL:		
Log in:		
Password/Pin:		
Notes/Hints/Security Question		

Title:	Password Change	Date
URL:		
Log in:		
Password/Pin:		
Notes/Hints/Security Question		

Title:	Password Change	Date
URL:		
Log in:		
Password/Pin:		
Notes/Hints/Security Question		

W

Title:	Password Change	Date
URL:		
Log in:		
Password/Pin:		
Notes/Hints/Security Question		

Title:	Password Change	Date
URL:		
Log in:		
Password/Pin:		
Notes/Hints/Security Question		

Title:	Password Change	Date
URL:		
Log in:		
Password/Pin:		
Notes/Hints/Security Question		

Title:	Password Change	Date
URL:		
Log in:		
Password/Pin:		
Notes/Hints/Security Question		

Title:	Password Change	Date
URL:		
Log in:		
Password/Pin:		
Notes/Hints/Security Question		

Title:	Password Change	Date
URL:		
Log in:		
Password/Pin:		
Notes/Hints/Security Question		

X

Title:	Password Change	Date
URL:		
Log in:		
Password/Pin:		
Notes/Hints/Security Question		

Title:	Password Change	Date
URL:		
Log in:		
Password/Pin:		
Notes/Hints/Security Question		

Title:	Password Change	Date
URL:		
Log in:		
Password/Pin:		
Notes/Hints/Security Question		

Title:	Password Change	Date
URL:		
Log in:		
Password/Pin:		
Notes/Hints/Security Question		

Title:	Password Change	Date
URL:		
Log in:		
Password/Pin:		
Notes/Hints/Security Question		

Title:	Password Change	Date
URL:		
Log in:		
Password/Pin:		
Notes/Hints/Security Question		

Y

Title:	Password Change	Date
URL:		
Log in:		
Password/Pin:		
Notes/Hints/Security Question		

Title:	Password Change	Date
URL:		
Log in:		
Password/Pin:		
Notes/Hints/Security Question		

Title:	Password Change	Date
URL:		
Log in:		
Password/Pin:		
Notes/Hints/Security Question		

Title:	Password Change	Date
URL:		
Log in:		
Password/Pin:		
Notes/Hints/Security Question		

Title:		Password Change	Date
URL:			
Log in:			
Password/Pin:			
Notes/Hints/Security Question			

Title:		Password Change	Date
URL:			
Log in:			
Password/Pin:			
Notes/Hints/Security Question			

Z

Title:	Password Change	Date
URL:		
Log in:		
Password/Pin:		
Notes/Hints/Security Question		

Title:	Password Change	Date
URL:		
Log in:		
Password/Pin:		
Notes/Hints/Security Question		

Title:	Password Change	Date
URL:		
Log in:		
Password/Pin:		
Notes/Hints/Security Question		

Title:	Password Change	Date
URL:		
Log in:		
Password/Pin:		
Notes/Hints/Security Question		

Title:	Password Change	Date
URL:		
Log in:		
Password/Pin:		
Notes/Hints/Security Question		

Title:	Password Change	Date
URL:		
Log in:		
Password/Pin:		
Notes/Hints/Security Question		

Internet Account

Internet Service Provider:
Account:
Password/Pin:
Tech Support:
Customer Service:

Back Up

Provider:
Log In/Account:
Password/Pin:

Provider:
Log In/Account:
Password/Pin:

Provider:
Log In/Account:
Password/Pin:

Email

Provider:	
Mail Server Type:	
Incoming Server:	
Outgoing Server:	
Username:	
Password/Pin:	
Password Change:	Dafe:
Password Change:	Dafe

Provider:	
Mail Server Type:	
Incoming Server:	
Outgoing Server:	
Username:	
Password/Pin:	
Password Change:	Dafe:
Password Change:	Dafe

Phone

Provider:	
Url:	
Account #:	
Phone #:	
Password/Pin:	
Password Change	**Date**

Provider:	
Url:	
Account #:	
Phone #:	
Password/Pin:	
Password Change	**Date**

Other

Internet Password Log Books Make Great Gifts

Here are some of our cover designs
-- including "Hide in Plain Sight" --
all available at Amazon.com and other retailers.

FastForwardPublishing.com

42387240R00052

Made in the USA
San Bernardino, CA
02 December 2016